D1288416

HorrorScapes

Dracula's Dark World

by Michael Burgan

Consultant: Michael Augustyn
Author of *Vlad Dracula: The Dragon Prince*

BEARPORT
PUBLISHING

New York, New York

Credits

Cover and Title Page, Illustration by Dawn Beard Creative and Kim Jones; 4–5, Kim Jones; 7L, Sir Simon Marsden/ Marsden Archive/SuperStock; 7R, © Apic/Getty Images; 9L, © Sandro Vannini/Corbis; 9R, © Tim E. White/Alamy; 10, Kim Jones; 11, © The Art Archive/SuperStock; 12, © Monica Wells PCL/SuperStock; 13, © Sir Simon Marsden/ Marsden Archive/SuperStock; 14, © Sir Simon Marsden/Marsden Archive/SuperStock; 15, © Georg Gerster/ Photo Researchers, Inc.; 16, Kim Jones; 17L, © Science and Society/SuperStock; 17R, © Georg Gerster/Photo Researchers, Inc.; 18, © Prisma/SuperStock; 19, Kim Jones; 20, © North Wind Picture Archives/Alamy; 21, © The Granger Collection, New York; 22, © Mary Evans Picture Library/Alamy; 23, © Bellini, Gentile (c.1429-1507)/The Art Gallery Collection/Alamy; 24, Kim Jones; 25, © Sir Simon Marsden/Marsden Archive/SuperStock; 26L, © Photos 12/ Alamy; 26R, © Front cover of 'Dracula' by Bram Stoker (1847-1912) 1920 (litho); Falke, Pierre (1884-1947)/Bibliothèque Nationale, Paris, France/Archives Charmet/The Bridgeman Art Library International; 27, © David Greedy/Getty Images; 28, © José Fuste Raga/age fotostock/SuperStock; 29, © Janet Wishnetsky/Imagestate Media Partners Limited-Impact Photos/Alamy; 32, © Lucertolone/Shutterstock.

Publisher: Kenn Goin
Editorial Director: Adam Siegel
Creative Director: Spencer Brinker
Design: Dawn Beard Creative and Kim Jones
Illustrations: Kim Jones
Photo Researcher: Picture Perfect Professionals, LLC

Library of Congress Cataloging-in-Publication Data

Burgan, Michael.
   Dracula's dark world / by Michael Burgan ; consultant, Michael Augustyn.
      p. cm. — (Horrorscapes)
   Includes bibliographical references and index.
   ISBN-13: 978-1-936087-96-9 (library binding)
   ISBN-10: 1-936087-96-0 (library binding)
   1. Vlad III, Prince of Wallachia, 1430 or 31-1476 or 7—Juvenile literature. 2. Wallachia—Kings and rulers—Biography—Juvenile literature. 3. Wallachia—History—15th century—Juvenile literature.
   4. Dracula, Count (Fictitious character)—Juvenile literature. I. Title.
   DR240.5.V553B87 2011
   949.8'2014092—dc22
   [B]
                                  2010014029

For more information, write to Bearport Publishing Company, Inc., 101 Fifth Avenue, Suite 6R, New York, New York 10003. Printed in the United States of America in North Mankato, Minnesota.

072010
042110CGF

10 9 8 7 6 5 4 3 2 1

Contents

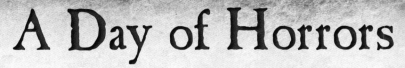

A Day of Horrors

The young **boyars** plodded past the palace of Prince Vlad Dracula. Their legs chained together, these rich and powerful men were his prisoners. The year was 1457. The boyars lived in Dracula's land of Wallachia (wah-LAY-kee-uh), a region of Romania. They were paying the price for angering their prince.

Just hours before, Dracula had killed dozens of older boyars and their wives. They had **betrayed** the prince when war broke out in Wallachia. Instead of helping Dracula's family, the boyars murdered his brother, Prince Mircea (MEERCH-yah). Dracula took his **revenge** by killing them in an especially cruel way—**impalement**. The prince had pointed stakes thrust into their bodies. The stakes were then placed outside the walls of the capital city of Tirgoviste (*ter*-guh-VEESH-tuh). Dracula wanted their painful deaths to warn others to always obey him.

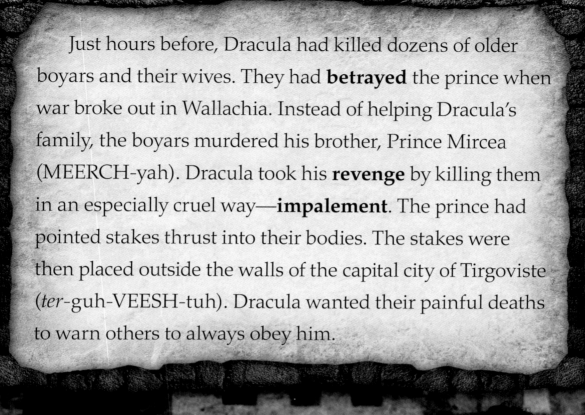

Impalement had been used to kill people for hundreds of years before Dracula came to power. However, Dracula impaled so many people that he earned the nickname Vlad Tepes (TSEH-pesh). The name is Romanian for "Vlad the Impaler."

Bloody Revenge

Dracula had other plans for the boyars and their families whom he did not impale. He marched them 50 miles (80 km) to Poenari (*poh*-yeh-NAR), an old **fortress** in northern Wallachia that sat high on a rocky hill. The prince hoped Poenari would protect him from anyone who might challenge his rule. There was one problem, however. The fortress lay in ruins. Prince Vlad would need many men to rebuild it. Luckily, he had the workers to do the mighty job.

This map shows Wallachia and neighboring lands in Dracula's time. Dracula ruled Wallachia three different times during his life.

Dracula's World

Sighisoara

Poenari Fortress

Tirgoviste

Arges River

Bucharest

Black Sea

- Transylvania
- Moldavia
- Wallachia
- - - Romania today

The boyars were now Dracula's slaves. They passed the tools and supplies they needed to rebuild the fortress from hand to hand. Others made bricks for Poenari's walls. Guards stood by, ready to whip anyone who slowed down. The job of rebuilding took months. Most of the boyars died from their back-breaking work. Yet in the end, Dracula had his fortress—and his revenge.

Much of Poenari Fortress was destroyed by earthquakes after Dracula's death. The remains of the fortress are shown here.

Vlad Dracula

According to **legend**, the boyars worked so hard that their clothes tore apart and fell off their weakened bodies.

Who Was Dracula?

Dracula came from a powerful family that had ruled in Wallachia for decades. His father, Prince Vlad II, had belonged to the Order of the Dragon. This small group of leaders promised to help stop the spread of non-Christian faiths. The greatest threat came from the Ottoman Turks. They had built an **Islamic empire** based in what is now Turkey. The Turks fought to spread their faith and **seize** new lands in parts of Europe.

After joining the Order of the Dragon, Vlad II was often called Dracul. The word means "dragon" in Romanian. *Dracula* means "son of the dragon." After Dracula began his bloody rule, people noted that *dracul* also means "devil."

The Ottoman Empire, 1453

Arctic Ocean

EUROPE · ASIA

NORTH AMERICA

Atlantic Ocean · AFRICA

Pacific Ocean

SOUTH AMERICA · Indian Ocean

AUSTRALIA

Southern Ocean

ANTARCTICA

Adriatic Sea

Black Sea

Mediterranean Sea

■ Ottoman Empire
--- Turkey today

During Dracula's life, the Ottoman Empire spread over parts of Asia and Europe.

Vlad II knew that the powerful Turks could crush his army. So he tried to stay friendly with the Turkish **sultan**. Yet in 1442, the sultan thought Vlad had betrayed him. Vlad had not offered any **military** help when the sultan was fighting a war in Europe. So the sultan captured Vlad and threw two of his sons, Dracula and Radu, into prison. After Vlad agreed to remain loyal to the sultan, he was released. His sons, however, remained in prison. Vlad had to obey the Turkish ruler if he wanted them to stay alive.

Many people believe this painting shows Dracula's father—Prince Vlad II.

Vlad II was living in this house in Sighisoara (*see*-gi-SHWAH-ruh), Transylvania, when his son Dracula was born around 1431.

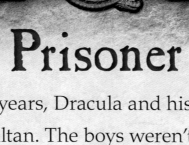

Prisoner

For almost six years, Dracula and his brother remained prisoners of the sultan. The boys weren't locked away in dark cells, however. Since they were **royalty**, the sultan treated them well. Still, the brothers knew their safety was always in danger if they did not follow orders.

Dracula and Radu received a good education during the years they were prisoners of the sultan. However, Dracula was sometimes whipped when he disobeyed his teachers.

By 1447, relations between Dracula's father and the sultan had improved. Now, however, Vlad II had a new enemy—the Hungarians. They wanted a distant member of Vlad's family, Vladislav II, to rule Wallachia. With just a few loyal boyars by his side, Vlad II prepared to battle his enemies. Unfortunately, he faced a much larger army. The enemy killed Vlad, chopping off his head with an ax.

As the year ended, Dracula heard both good and bad news. He was free to return home—but his father was dead. So was his brother Mircea, who had been buried alive by disloyal boyars. His family no longer ruled in Wallachia. Dracula would have to fight to win back his **throne**.

When he received his freedom, Dracula briefly served in the Turkish army. He joined knowing he would soon need Turkish help to rule Wallachia.

Murad (moo-RAHD) II was the Turkish sultan who captured Dracula. The sultans of this era usually killed their own brothers so they could not challenge the sultans' power.

The Road to Rule

Enemies waited for Dracula back in Wallachia. The new prince there, Vladislav II, and the Hungarians did not want Dracula to rule. Dracula, however, had other ideas. He returned to Wallachia with an army. Vladislav was away at the time, fighting in another part of Europe. The troops left behind were too weak to challenge Dracula's forces and he seized the throne. Vladislav, however, soon returned with his huge army. To stay alive, Vlad fled. His rule had lasted just a few months.

After escaping from Wallachia, Dracula spent time in the Transylvanian town of Sibiu (see-BYOO).

In the years that followed, the Hungarians became upset with Vladislav. They didn't like the way he ruled. So they turned against him and made peace with Dracula. With Hungarian support, Dracula formed a new army. During the summer of 1456, he defeated Vladislav's forces and won back his throne. Dracula had learned how rulers must act to survive. Friendships end and **alliances** switch quickly. Dracula would always do what was best for himself and act strongly against his enemies.

By one account, Dracula killed Vladislav II in hand-to-hand combat. The murder was partly revenge for Dracula, since Vladislav had played a role in the death of Dracula's father.

This statue of Dracula, showing him as a mighty ruler, stands in Tirgoviste, Romania.

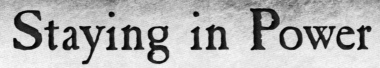

Staying in Power

Now in power, Dracula began his war against the boyars who had killed his brother and opposed his rule. One boyar named Albu raised an army to challenge Dracula. The prince's army captured it. Dracula then impaled everyone in Albu's family, including the women and children. He did not want any of the relatives to one day seek revenge against him.

Dracula used this tower at Tirgoviste to watch impalements. It was rebuilt during the 1800s.

During his early years as prince, Dracula often spent time at Poenari. The stone walls of the fortress were extra thick, so invading armies could not destroy it with cannons. Dracula's fortress also had five round towers. From them, his soldiers could fire down on enemy attackers.

The Arges River

Legends say Dracula built a secret tunnel from the fortress at Poenari to the Arges (AR-jesh) River. If enemies were able to enter the fortress, he could use the tunnel to escape.

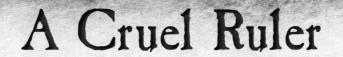

A Cruel Ruler

Dracula had no concern for the sick, the poor, or others who did not work. One day, he called them all to Tirgoviste for a huge feast. As blind men and beggars joyfully ate and drank, Dracula's soldiers nailed shut the doors to their dining hall. Then they set the building on fire. Flames soared to the sky as the dying diners moaned and shrieked inside.

Despite Dracula's cruel ways, many peasants liked him. The harsh punishments he gave criminals, such as impalement, reduced crime. He gave some peasants land and cut taxes for some villages. In addition, Dracula believed in enforcing law and order. Rich criminals could not escape jail by paying money to the court. This **bribery** had been common in the past.

Rulers in Dracula's time counted on peasants to cut down trees and grow crops.

Dracula was clever as well as cruel. At times, the prince **disguised** himself as a common man and rode through the country. He wanted to make sure everyone was working hard.

Wallachia is still known for its excellent farmlands.

Slaughter of the Saxons

Dracula's bloody acts went beyond his own land. Germans called Saxons had settled in nearby Transylvania. Some Saxons supported Dan III, a relative of Dracula's, as the true ruler of Wallachia. Starting in 1457, an angry Dracula led soldiers into southern Transylvania. They destroyed several Saxon towns. A Saxon later wrote that people were "hacked to pieces like cabbage" by Dracula's army. Dracula sent other Saxons back to Tirgoviste to be impaled.

Dracula's palace at Tirgoviste included a torture chamber. In such rooms, rulers sometimes tightly squeezed prisoners' thumbs in wooden presses or stretched the prisoners on racks that tore arms and legs from their bodies.

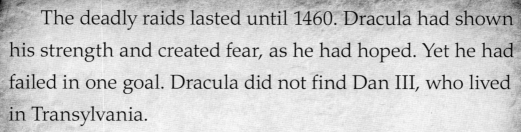

The deadly raids lasted until 1460. Dracula had shown his strength and created fear, as he had hoped. Yet he had failed in one goal. Dracula did not find Dan III, who lived in Transylvania.

Starting late in 1459, Dan had begun to raise an army to invade Wallachia. The next spring, he met Dracula's forces along the border. The battle went badly for Dan. Dracula's men killed almost all his soldiers. Dracula forced Dan to dig his own grave. According to legend, the prince then killed Dan by cutting off his head.

In at least one Saxon town, Dracula placed some prisoners in a huge metal pot. He had the pot filled with water and then lit a fire under it. The prisoners were soon boiled alive.

Reporting the Horrors of Dracula

Not all the Saxons died in pots or on posts. Some escaped and reported what they saw. The tales were not just told from one person to another. A few years before Dracula first came to power, Johannes Gutenberg (*yoh*-HAHN-*uhss* GOOT-uhn-*burg*) of Germany built Europe's first printing press. German printers later published the horrible stories about Dracula. Some of the **pamphlets** also had pictures of the bloody deaths he had caused.

This is the kind of printing press that was used to spread the story of Dracula across Europe.

Historians know of at least **13** pamphlets about Dracula published between **1488** and **1521**. One of them is called *The Frightening and Truly Extraordinary Story of a Wicked Blood-drinking Tyrant Called Prince Dracula*.

Many of the details about Dracula's life were true. Yet some printers also stretched the truth. They wanted to make Dracula seem like a blood-crazed madman. Some writers hoped to weaken support for Dracula in Wallachia. Others hated him for what he had done to the Saxons. Still, readers enjoyed these bloody tales.

According to legend, Dracula calmly ate a meal while surrounded by impaled Saxons.

Battling the Turks

Dracula's actions in Transylvania secured his power in Wallachia. Yet the Ottoman Empire was still a threat. The new sultan, Mehmed (meh-MEHT) II, wanted more European lands—including those where Dracula ruled.

In 1462, Mehmed led a huge army of Turkish soldiers into Wallachia. Dracula chose to escape rather than fight directly. As he left, he created as much damage as he could. He burned crops and poisoned **wells** in Wallachia so the Turks would not have food and water.

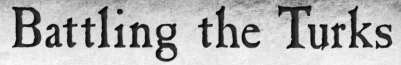
This drawing shows Turkish soldiers in battle during the late 1400s.

To scare the Turks and weaken their will to fight, Dracula set up a "forest of the impaled." He left about 20,000 rotting bodies on posts outside Tirgoviste. The dead included captured soldiers, women, and children.

Mehmed eventually gave up the chase and returned to his empire. In his place he left Dracula's brother Radu to rule Wallachia. Radu and the sultan were friends. He would follow the Turks' orders.

As Radu took power, Dracula fled to Poenari. Turkish troops that helped Radu followed Dracula there and surrounded the castle. Before the Turks could attack, however, he managed to slip safely away.

Mehmed II, pictured here, was the son of Murad II, who had held Dracula and Radu prisoner years before.

Prison, Prince Again, Death

Dracula fled to Transylvania. He waited there to meet Matthias Corvinus (muh-THYE-uhss kor-VYE-nuhss), the king of Hungary. Dracula wanted his help in battling the Turks. Instead, Matthias had him arrested. Someone had **forged** Dracula's name on papers. They falsely claimed Dracula was going to help the Turks fight Hungary. Dracula spent the next 12 years as the king's prisoner.

Dracula may have impaled more than his enemies. Several stories say that when he was in prison he asked guards to bring him birds and mice so that he could impale them on tiny wooden stakes.

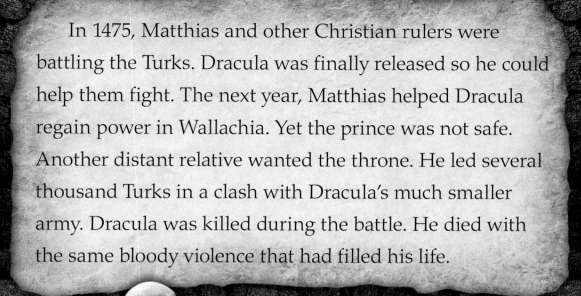

In 1475, Matthias and other Christian rulers were battling the Turks. Dracula was finally released so he could help them fight. The next year, Matthias helped Dracula regain power in Wallachia. Yet the prince was not safe. Another distant relative wanted the throne. He led several thousand Turks in a clash with Dracula's much smaller army. Dracula was killed during the battle. He died with the same bloody violence that had filled his life.

Dracula was said to be buried in Snagov (SNAH-gohv), Wallachia. Digging at the site in 1931 revealed only a few animal bones. Today, no one knows for sure where Dracula is buried.

The chapel in Snagov where Dracula's body may be buried

Count Dracula

After his death, Dracula's violent ways were soon forgotten by much of the world. During the 1890s, however, the author Bram Stoker learned about the violent prince. Stoker was writing a **novel** about a **vampire** when he first read about Dracula. Although he decided to name his vampire Count Dracula, there is no proof that Stoker knew all the gory details of Vlad's life.

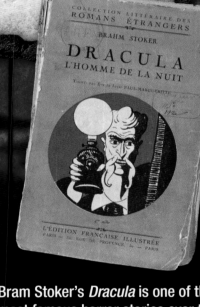

Bram Stoker's *Dracula* is one of the most famous horror stories ever told.

Count Dracula as he appeared in a 1931 film based on Stoker's book

More than 160 films feature a character based on Bram Stoker's Count Dracula.

Still, the book *Dracula* made some people curious about the real Dracula. They wondered if Stoker had based his character on the prince. Was the real Dracula a vampire? After all, one old tale about the Saxons said Dracula "dipped his bread in the blood of his victims."

The truth, of course, is that Prince Vlad had not been a vampire. Instead, he had been a ruler who used violence to win and keep power. However, there is one important way in which the two Draculas are the same. Whether in the novel or in real life, many people felt safe only when they knew for sure that Dracula was dead.

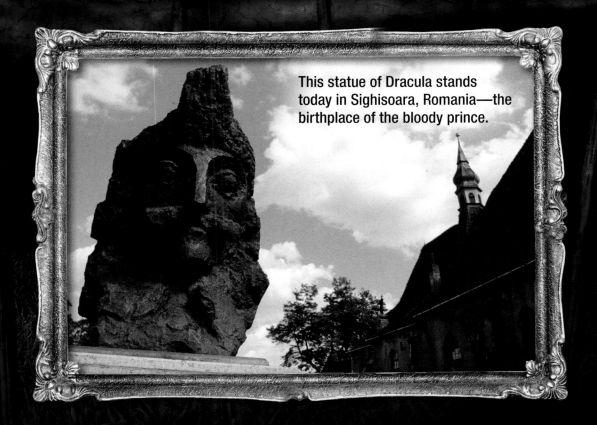

This statue of Dracula stands today in Sighisoara, Romania—the birthplace of the bloody prince.

DRACULA'S WORLD:
Then and Now

Then: Romania was made up of several different countries ruled by princes. The power to rule usually stayed within one family.

Now: Romania is one united country with a government elected by the people. The president of the country is elected every five years.

Then: Tirgoviste was the capital of Dracula's Wallachia.

Now: Bucharest, in Wallachia, is the capital of Romania. It has a population of around two million people.

The city of Bucharest was first mentioned in written records while Dracula ruled Wallachia, more than 500 years ago. Today, Bucharest is the largest city in Romania.

Then: The Ottoman Empire stretched from the modern nation of Georgia to modern-day Greece.

Now: The Ottoman Empire lasted until 1922. By then, it had lost much of its lands after fighting on the losing side in World War I (1914–1918). The remaining Turkish land became the Republic of Turkey—which still exists today.

Then: Several of Dracula's Romanian relatives ruled Wallachia after his death, including a son and a grandson.

Now: Members of a family with the last name Drakula claim to be directly related to Dracula. Some live in Europe and others live in the United States.

Along the Arges River, 1,400 steps lead to what remains of Poenari Fortress.

Glossary

alliances (uh-LYE-uhnss-iz) agreements between people or nations to help one another, especially during wartime

betrayed (bi-TRAYD) broke a promise or turned against a friend or ruler

boyars (boh-YARZ) rich and powerful landowners who lived in parts of Eastern Europe

bribery (BRYE-bur-ee) the act of offering money or a gift to get someone to do something that is usually wrong

disguised (diss-GYEZD) dressed as someone else to fool others

empire (EHM-pye-ur) a group of countries or regions ruled by a single person

forged (FORJD) wrongfully signed another person's name on a paper

fortress (FOR-triss) a strong building from which people can defend an area

impalement (im-PAYL-muhnt) driving a sharp wooden pole through a person's body

Islamic (iz-LAH-mik) relating to the religion of Islam, whose followers are called Muslims

legend (LEJ-uhnd) a story that is handed down from the past that may be based on fact but is not always completely true

military (MIL-uh-*ter*-ee) having to do with armies or soldiers

novel (NOV-uhl) a book that tells a long made-up story

pamphlets (PAM-flits) small books with soft covers

revenge (ri-VENJ) punishment for something that has been unfairly done

royalty (ROY-uhl-tee) kings, queens, princesses, and princes

seize (SEEZ) grab hold of; take by force

sultan (SUHL-tuhn) the ruler in some Muslim countries

throne (THROHN) the chair used by a ruler, or the power the ruler holds

vampire (VAM-*pye*-ur) in stories, a dead person who rises from the grave to suck the blood of living people

wells (WELZ) deep holes dug in the ground to get water

Bibliography

Florescu, Radu R., and Raymond T. McNally. *Dracula, Prince of Many Faces: His Life and Times.* Boston: Little, Brown and Company (1989).

Florescu, Radu R., and Raymond T. McNally. *In Search of Dracula: The History of Dracula and Vampires.* Boston: Houghton Mifflin (1994).

Klepper, Nicolae. *Romania: An Illustrated History.* New York: Hippocrene Books (2002).

Rezachevici, Constantin. "From the Order of the Dragon to Dracula." *Journal of Dracula Studies,* Vol. 1 (1999).

Treptow, Kurt W., ed. *Dracula: Essays on the Life and Times of Vlad Tepes.* New York: Columbia University Press (1991).

Read More

Goldberg, Enid A., and Norman Itzkowitz. *Vlad the Impaler: The Real Count Dracula.* New York: Franklin Watts (2008).

Van Cleaf, Kristin. *Romania.* Edina, MN: ABDO Publishing (2008).

Learn More Online

To learn more about Prince Vlad Dracula and his world, visit
www.bearportpublishing.com/HorrorScapes

Index

About the Author

Michael Burgan has written more than 200 books for children about history, science, and sports. One of these was a graphic novel version of Bram Stoker's *Dracula*. He lives in West Haven, Connecticut, with his wife and cat.